Baptist Identity Series
LEADER'S GUIDE FOR GROUP STUDY

Suggestions for Persons Leading Groups Studying
the Baptist Identity Leaflets and *Personal Study Guides*

William M. Pinson, Jr.
Doris A. Tinker
with
Dennis A. Parrott ~ Skyler G. Tinker

Baptist Identity Series
LEADER'S GUIDE FOR GROUP STUDY

Baptist Identity Series
A resource from the Texas Baptist Heritage Center
William M. Pinson, Jr., Director
Doris A. Tinker, Director of Communications/Organization

Scripture quotations marked NIV are taken from the Holy Bible, New International Version,
Copyright © 1973, 1978, 1984 by the International Bible Society.
The King James Version is used in all other scripture quotations; it has been
widely used for centuries and is familiar to many generations.
Many other versions and translations are available.

Printed in the United States of America

First Edition: 2014
ISBN-13: 978-1-934741-24-5
ISBN-10:   1-934741-24-8

Table of Contents

A Word of Introduction

As the leader of a study group, you play a key role in what is learned and how the learning is applied. What an opportunity! What a responsibility!

Whether you have led many group studies or this is your first, you can count on the experience to be a learning one for you as well as for the members of the group. We pray that the experience will be a very positive one for all of those involved.

A Description of the *Baptist Identity Series*

The *Baptist Identity Series* consists of these items: (1) *Baptist Beliefs and Heritage*, a book containing nineteen colorful 4-page leaflets on Baptist beliefs and practices, insights on key words and terms, brief information on Baptist individuals and events, and a summary history of Baptists [the leaflets are also available in packets that contain the nineteen leaflets in a 4-page 5.5 x 8.5 format], (2) *Personal Study Guides*, a book containing nineteen study guides on the leaflets for use by individuals in personal study and in a group study, and (3) *Leader's Guide for Group Study*, (this book) that contains nineteen study guides on each of the leaflets and a section on Suggestions for Leaders of Group Study. The topics for the nineteen leaflets are listed on the Table of Contents page.

The Significance of This Study

The purpose of the *Baptist Identity Series* is to strengthen the Baptist family of Christians and to help develop more dedicated, equipped servants of Jesus Christ to carry out his mission in our world. How members of the group apply the content of this study will affect not only their lives but also the ministry of Baptist churches, institutions, and other organizations—and even the condition of society.

The Importance of Group Study

Research has shown that people learn and apply information best when they go through three stages: (1) They read about or listen to someone present the information. (2) They undertake some learning exercises on their own in order to better understand the material. (3) They engage in a group discussion with others who are studying the same material, ideally with the guidance of a group leader.

The nineteen leaflets in the *Baptist Identity Series* relate to stage one; they provide the basic information on each topic. The *Personal Study Guides* book relates to stage two; it provides learning exercises to further the understanding of each topic. The *Leader's Guide for Group Study* (this book) relates to stage three; it is a resource to help you, as a group leader, to facilitate discussion and application of each topic.

5

Suggestions for the Group Study

Each group has its own personality, and thus there is no way for any leader's guide to cover all of the possibilities. This book is designed to help you prepare for and conduct the group meetings. However, it is only a help. As a group leader, prayer, careful preparation, and knowledge not only of the material to be studied but also of the members of the group are keys to a good learning experience.

Similarly, each leader of a group is a distinct personality and will approach the role in keeping with his or her background, experience, and relation with the group. Therefore, you will develop the group study in your own unique way. The material in this book is adaptable to be individualized by the group leader. And, of course, you may decide on an approach that is very different from what is suggested here.

Possible Questions for This Study

Some questions may come from members of the group about the study itself, such as these: Why was the *Series* developed? What qualifications do the authors of the material have? How can the *Series* be used by individuals, churches, and other organizations? The basic answers to these questions are found in the *Personal Study Guides* book on pages 86 and 87, as well as on pages 56 and 57 in this book. You may find it helpful to deal with such questions as part of the beginning of the group discussion. Additional questions may arise, such as the following:

1. Is the *Series* an official statement of Baptist beliefs? No, it is not. The material in the *Baptist Identity Series* does not purport to present an "official" Baptist statement on any of the topics. Baptists do not have any such "official" statement. The authors are solely responsible for the content of the *Series* and have endeavored to set forth beliefs and polities commonly held by Baptists.

2. How do Baptist beliefs and practices compare with or differ from those of other Christian groups? The *Series* was not designed to deal specifically with such comparisons. You might suggest that persons interested in the differences and similarities can find resources in a variety of places that set forth the beliefs and practices of other Christian denominations. Clearly, Baptists have many beliefs and practices in common with other parts of the Christian community even while being a distinct denomination.

3. Since Baptists have much in common with other Christian groups, what sets them apart as distinct? As Leaflet 2, *Baptists: What Makes a Baptist a Baptist?*, explains, no single belief sets Baptists apart as a distinct group, but rather it is a combination or recipe of beliefs. Keep in mind that the intent of the *Series* is not to put down the beliefs of others but rather to hold up the beliefs and practices of Baptists.

4. Why study about the Baptist denomination rather than about what it means to be a Christian? Studying what it means to be a Christian is always of vital importance. However, the study of a denomination is also important. For one thing, to strengthen the Baptist denomination is one means of strengthening the Christian movement worldwide. A means of strengthening the denomination is by helping Baptists to be thoroughly aware of and committed to the beliefs and polities which enable it to function effectively in missions, evangelism, Christian education, and ministry.

5. Are denominations really significant? Some persons feel that denominations are bad or out of date. They may not be aware of the multiple millions of persons who are part of Christian denominations, the continued growth of a number of denominations, and the vast, varied ministries conducted by denominations, all of which indicate the importance of denominations. You may find it helpful to spend some of the opening session discussing such matters as the definition of a denomination, the distinction between a denomination and the organizations related to it, and the many positive contributions of denominations in general and of the Baptist denomination in particular.

6. What is the history of the Baptist denomination? The *Baptist Identity Series* does not major on the history of Baptists although certainly the content of the leaflets in the *Series* on the beliefs, polity, and practices of Baptists relates to the history of Baptists. Persons interested in studying Baptist history will find helpful resources listed on the website www.baptistdistinctives.org. Also, the book *Baptist Beliefs and Heritage*, which is part of the *Baptist Identity Series*, contains a brief summary of Baptist history as well as brief biographical sketches of several Baptists and information on particular events in the Baptist story.

7. What is the relationship of the nineteen leaflets in the *Baptist Identity Series* to the twenty-seven articles on the website www.baptistdistinctives.org? The articles were printed each week over a period of a year in a Baptist newspaper and posted on the website. Many persons requested that the material in the articles be put into leaflet format, and this was done. The leaflets, both text and graphics, are based on the articles.

Conclusion

As the leader of a study group, you are part of a company of other group leaders. Pray for these other leaders and groups that the studies will advance the cause of Christ under the guidance of the Holy Spirit to the glory of God the Father.

We pray that you will have a very
positive, rewarding experience
leading the group study.

Enjoy the experience and
endeavor to make it constructive
for all of those who are involved.

Suggestions for Leaders of Group Study

This book provides resources for persons who lead groups in studying the leaflets in the *Baptist Identity Series*. If you are experienced in leading group discussions, you will already be familiar with many, perhaps all, of these suggestions and quite possibly have your own approach. If you are a newcomer to leading such groups, hopefully these resources will be helpful to you.

> The *Baptist Identity Series* leaflets and study guides fit especially well for use with groups of Baptists who are members of the same local church. However, the study guides can be adapted with ease to the particular makeup of a wide variety of different types of groups.

In this book you will find general suggestions for leading a group study and also specific suggestions for studying each of the nineteen leaflets in the *Series*. Of course, you may choose to follow closely these suggestions, adjust them, or take an entirely different approach according to your preference and the makeup of the group. No leader's guide will fit every leader or every group.

The following suggestions are organized into three parts: (1) General Suggestions for Preparing to Lead the Group Study, (2) Specific Suggestions for Preparation Prior to Each Group Session, and (3) Suggestions for Leading Group Studies.

General Suggestions for Preparing to Lead the Group Study

Your preparation to lead a group study will depend, for one thing, on the characteristics of the group. You will need to develop your approach according to the nature and size of the group. Groups may vary in myriad ways, such as the number of persons in the group, the age of the participants, the degree of knowledge about Baptist beliefs and practices, and the level of interest in the subject matter by the group members.

> Adapt these guides to your particular group and your own style of leadership. Groups differ; leaders are unique. Remember that no study guide will fit all.

As the leader of a group studying the *Baptist Identity Series* leaflets, you will need the book *Baptist Beliefs and Heritage* and the book *Personal Study Guides*. Information on ordering each of these is found on the How to Order Materials page in the back of this book. You will find it helpful to become familiar with all of the leaflets as well as the material in the *Personal Study Guides* book for each leaflet. For maximum effectiveness see that each member of the group has a copy of the *Baptist Beliefs and Heritage* book and the *Personal Study Guides* book **prior to** the first group meeting. The group will find it convenient to have **all** of the leaflets bound in one book and will find the additional information on each leaflet helpful in the study. Regarding payment for the cost of the materials, each participant might pay for his or her own materials, or the cost might be covered by the sponsoring entity, such as your church. Effort has been made to see that the cost of the materials is basically just the printing cost. Financial assistance from persons interested in making the *Series* available, the utilization of skilled professionals who volunteered their time, and the fact that the authors donated their service all contributed to this effort.

The location of the group study will also affect the preparation for and nature of each session. Make sure that the space and facilities available will be appropriate for the group.

By the Way . . .

In preparing to lead a group session, a good way to study would be to have at hand the leaflet(s), the *Personal Study Guides* book, and the *Leader's Guide for Group Study* book. Read the leaflet(s). Do the activities in the *Personal Study Guides* book. Study carefully the suggestions for leading the group in the *Leader's Guide for Group Study* book.

Determining the number of sessions that you will have for the group study will depend on several factors, such as how many of the topics will be dealt with and the setting for the study. Ideally, all nineteen leaflets will be studied. However, it is possible to deal with only selected topics.

If you will be studying all nineteen of the leaflets, the topics can be grouped in ways to provide a satisfactory study for various settings, such as a Sunday School class or a retreat. Whatever grouping is decided on, consider combining Leaflet 1 and Leaflet 2 for the first session since they are more or less introductory. Here are a few examples of ways to group the topics when all nineteen are to be studied:

One way would be to have an introductory session (Leaflet 1 and Leaflet 2) followed by a session on each of the remaining leaflets for a total of eighteen sessions. This type of grouping could be applied to a variety of settings for the study.

For a quarter of a year in a Sunday School study, which would likely be approximately twelve sessions, you might group the topics as follows: Session One, Leaflets 1 and 2; Session Two, Leaflet 3; Session Three, Leaflet 4; Session Four, Leaflets 5, 6, and 7; Session Five, Leaflets 8 and 9; Session Six, Leaflets 10 and 11; Session Seven, Leaflet 12; Session Eight, Leaflet 13;

Session Nine, Leaflets 14 and 15; Session Ten, Leaflets 16 and 18; Session Eleven, Leaflet 17; Session Twelve, Leaflet 19.

If the study will be once a week for a month, such as conducted during a weekday, Sunday afternoons or nights, or on Wednesday nights, you might group the topics as follows: Session One, Leaflets 1-4; Session Two, Leaflets 5-10; Session Three, Leaflets 11-13; Session Four, Leaflets 14-19.

Specific Suggestions for Preparation Prior to Each Group Session

In addition to general preparation for the group study, some specific things can be done prior to each session that will enhance the effectiveness of the study.

- Pray for the study to be helpful for the participants and to contribute to the advancement of the cause of Christ.

- Arrange the meeting place for effective group participation. The arrangement will depend to some degree on what method of group study will be utilized. For example, the arrangement for a lecture approach may differ from that for a discussion approach. If you plan to divide the group into smaller groups for discussion, be sure that the facilities are adequate for this. See that the temperature is comfortable and the lighting is satisfactory.

- Consider gathering for display related materials on the topic for each session, such as photographs, magazine articles, newspaper clippings, and possibly items printed from the Internet.

- Make certain that you have available all of the resources you will need for the session, such as a table for display of materials and equipment for learning aids that you plan to utilize.

- Determine if you want to use teaching/learning activities, such as role play, skits, guest speakers, or a panel discussion, and if you do, make adequate preparation ahead of time.

- Ask that each participant, if possible prior to the time of the group session, read the leaflet(s), focus on the scripture(s), and fill in the blanks and consider the application questions in the *Personal Study Guides* book on the leaflet topic(s) to be considered. Ask each person to bring a Bible and something with which to take notes.

- Develop the key idea, the session goal, and the application to life for each session and put these in writing. You may want to share these with the group at the beginning of the session. In the box at the top of the following page is a suggested example related to Leaflet 2.

Baptists: What Makes a Baptist a Baptist?

Key Idea: No single belief or practice identifies Baptists as Baptists but rather a recipe or collection of basic beliefs and practices.

Session Goal: That the members of the group will know the ingredients of the Baptist Recipe and begin to understand why Baptists through the ages have felt that these are worth suffering and even dying for.

Application to Life: Consider how you can enhance gratitude for the Baptist Recipe in your church, among other Baptists, and among non-Baptists.

Plan the session carefully to fit the allotted time but also be flexible. For example, in some instances the interest may be especially high and the discussions run long so that you do not finish what you have planned; consider carrying the topic over until the next session. In other instances, you may complete what you have planned before the time the session is over; you might consider being prepared to begin the presentation of the next topic if the group study is covering several or all of the topics in the *Baptist Identity Series*.

In your planning think through how you want to utilize the suggestions in this book for guiding the group study on each leaflet. The suggestions that are included in the following pages are organized into four sections in each of the nineteen study guides: **(1) Getting Started**, **(2) Guiding the Group Study**, **(3) Closing**, and **(4) Prayer Time**.

Prior to the first group session, read carefully all of the leaflets that you will be dealing with in the sessions. (The topics covered by the nineteen leaflets are listed on the Table of Contents page of this book.) This will enable you to relate each topic as it is studied to the others as you progress through the group study sessions. For additional resources on each leaflet, see www.baptistdistinctives.org and/or check for available materials in a library or on the Internet.

Suggestions for Leading Group Studies

If you are experienced in leading group studies, you may consider the following information superfluous. However, it might be useful for review. If this is your first experience as a leader of a group, you will hopefully find these ideas helpful—but not nearly complete! Every group experience is different, as is every group study. We really are all learners when it comes to leading groups. Here are a few hints for effective group studies:

• Get to know about the members of the group before the first meeting. The characteristics of the individuals and of the group as a whole will play a big role in how you relate to the group as its leader. For example, if all of the members know one another very well, the approach will be different than if the members are strangers to each other. Groups of teenagers function differently than groups of older adults. Groups of longtime, knowledgeable Baptists will function on the topic of Baptist identity differently than groups of persons who are either new to Baptist life or know little about it.

- At times, a suggested question for discussion may call for an opinion. It may not have a right or wrong answer as such. You might consider phrasing such questions in this way: "What do you think about…?" or "What is your opinion about…?"

- If a discussion question calls for a factual answer, be prepared to provide the answer in case no one in the group knows it.

- If you are asked a question about something that you or no one in the group has an answer for, indicate that you will try to find the answer before the next meeting of the group, or you might request a group member to research the question and bring a report.

- In the first meeting of the group, you might outline some guidelines for the discussion periods. This would not be necessary in some groups, but it could be a good thing to do ahead of time for others. Listing guidelines such as the following on a poster or in some other visual way might be helpful:

    Everyone is to have an opportunity to participate in discussions, but no one is to be required to do so.

    Respect the opinion of others.

    Avoid interrupting others while they are speaking.

    Read the leaflets and do the activities in the *Personal Study Guides* in advance.

    Bring a Bible and items for making notes.

- As appropriate, affirm the members of the group for their preparation and participation.

Guides for Leaders
of Group Study

Each of the following nineteen guides for leaders of group study contains suggestions for the group study organized around four sections found in all of the study guides: Getting Started, Guiding the Group Study, Closing, and Prayer Time. Here are some suggestions for the utilization of material in each of these sections:

Getting Started. In each Getting Started section, the group is encouraged to commit a scripture to memory that is related to the leaflet being studied. The *Personal Study Guides* book contains suggestions for memorizing scripture. You might want to utilize these suggestions in the group time. Use the translation of the scripture that is in the leaflets and study guides so that all of the members will be using the same translation when quoting and memorizing the scriptures. In a few instances only a portion of the scripture referenced is printed for memorization.

Scripture memory is an important aspect of a Christian's life. God's Word committed to memory is available to us to recall at any time in our lives in all of life's circumstances.

You will also find in the Getting Started section suggestions for introducing the topic and focusing attention on it.

Guiding the Group Study. In the Guiding the Group Study section, you will find suggestions for each of the subheadings of the leaflet. A discussion approach is assumed. If for whatever reason the group does not lend itself to a discussion approach or you as the group leader prefer another approach, carefully plan an alternative, such as a lecture approach.

Case studies are included in the leader's guide for several of the sessions. They are not in the *Personal Study Guides* book. These are intended to help initiate discussion on the topic as you share them with the group. Although the case studies are based on actual events, the description in each is hypothetical. In some instances there is no right or wrong answer as such, but the group is encouraged to consider options and possibilities.

Closing. The Closing section usually contains discussion questions to help focus on the topic of the session and also utilizes the *Personal Study Guides* book's Fill in the Blanks and Application Questions. Answers to the Fill in the Blanks are found in the *Personal Study Guides* book. In regard to Application Questions, you will likely not have time to deal with all of these. Select the ones that you want to discuss or ask the group which one or ones they want to discuss. If the group session is one of a series, briefly review the previous session(s) and preview the session(s) to come.

By the Way . . .

The Closing section in the group meeting affords opportunity to review the topic with special attention given to how it can be applied to life. Knowing facts and acquiring information is well and good, but the proof of a successful session is that the members apply to life what they have learned. You might ask yourself, "How will my own life be different because of this study?"

Prayer Time. The nature of the Prayer Time will be determined to a large degree by the characteristics of the group, such as size, age, and church involvement. This time will help to enable the group members to end the session in a positive, devotional manner.

Of course, you will want to adapt these suggestions to fit the group and your own style of leading groups. As you know, you do not need to use all of the suggestions. The number of these suggestions that you utilize will depend on such matters as the total time provided for the session, the level of involvement by members in the discussion, and the nature of the group.

There is some repetition in the study guides material because each study guide is designed to stand alone, and thus some information is repeated in each.

Note: The suggested questions for discussion are not enclosed in quotation marks. Instead they are introduced by the word Ask, that is followed by the question beginning with a capital letter. Example: Ask, Where is the water fountain?

Learning Aids for Guiding the Group Study

Some of the study guides suggest interactive discussion where members' comments are to be listed in a format that is large enough for all to see. The method of displaying these comments will be determined by several factors, such as resources available and your preference as group leader. Marker boards, poster boards, or large sheets of paper are readily available, inexpensive, and suitable for use in small groups. However, you may prefer to utilize any of the available technologies that would be conducive for the particular setting of the group that you will be guiding for the study. New technologies are continually emerging for use as excellent learning resources.

A worthy goal in leading a successful group study is for each member of the group to apply to life~personal, family, church, community~what they have studied and learned.

The following guides have been developed to help achieve that goal.

Baptists
Who? Where? What? Why?

The following suggestions for leaders of group study are based on Baptist Identity Leaflet No. 1.

Scripture Memory

"Yea, I have a goodly heritage." Psalm 16:6

Getting Started

Begin the meeting with prayer. If this is the first meeting of the group, request each person to introduce herself or himself if the members do not know one another. For the group study, the members will need copies of the Baptist Identity Leaflets, either in the *Baptist Beliefs and Heritage* book or as individual leaflets, as well as the *Personal Study Guides* book. Arrange for the members to have these in advance of the first meeting if possible; if not, have copies for them at the meeting.

Read in unison Psalm 16:6 printed in the Scripture Memory section above that is also printed in the leaflet and in the *Personal Study Guides* book. Lead the group in memorizing this scripture.

Indicate that many Baptists have made major contributions to the Christian movement and to society, but often they are not known or are not known as being Baptists. As an indication of this, review the answers to the "Did you know that..." list in the leaflet.

Ask, Why do you think that many persons, including many Baptists, do not know a great deal about Baptist heritage, beliefs, and practices? Do you think that the general impression about Baptists by non-Baptists is positive or negative? Why?

Guiding the Group Study

Lead a discussion on each of the subsections of the leaflet. Here are some suggested discussion starters, or you may choose to develop your own.

Who Are Baptists? Read the list of Baptist diversities printed in the leaflet, and after each one is read, request the group to name at least one Baptist, past or present, who represents this diversity. [Note: Be prepared to name one in case the group cannot.]

Where Are Baptists Found? Ask, Why do you think that there is such a large concentration of Baptists in North America, particularly in the United States of America? In what ways do some of the major beliefs of Baptists fit with the beliefs and values that characterized early Americans as they established and expanded the nation? [Hint: a commitment to individual responsibility, freedom, and faith in God]

17

What Are the Contributions of Baptists? Using some method that can be easily viewed by the whole group, write: "Contributions of Baptists." Indicate that Baptists are interested in meeting the total needs of persons, such as spiritual, physical, emotional, social, and mental. Request members of the group to name contributions by Baptists, and as each contribution is named, list it. [Examples: worship services; food and clothes closets for needy persons; support groups for those with special needs, such as those grieving the death of a loved one; literacy training; evangelistic meetings; recreation and athletic programs; institutions to care for neglected and abused children; counseling; hospitals; schools; response to disasters, such as floods, earthquakes, hurricanes, and tornadoes; efforts for religious freedom for all]

After a number of contributions have been listed, request members to indicate which of these are available locally? Place the letter "L" by the contributions that are named. Then request persons to share which of these they have had personal experience with as a participant, contributor, or beneficiary. Place the letter "P" by the contributions as they are named.

Why Do Baptists Function as They Do? Using the same method as above, make three columns headed "Basic Doctrines," "Basic Polities," and "Basic Practices and Emphases." Briefly summarize the distinctions between doctrines, polities, and basic practices and emphases. Request the members to state items that go under each heading, using the leaflet as a source. Indicate that the leaflets in the *Baptist Identity Series* deal with each of these which taken as a whole help define Baptists. Lead a discussion on how each of these doctrines, polities, practices, and emphases shapes Baptist life.

Closing

Request members to share what, if anything, new they have learned about Baptists from this study. Request persons to volunteer to share which one of the doctrines, polities, practices, or emphases is especially meaningful to him or her. Ask, How can you apply one or more of these in your life to contribute to the effectiveness of Baptist ministry in Christ's name? Lead the members of the group in reviewing the Fill in the Blanks section and the Application Questions in the *Personal Study Guides* book.

Prayer Time

Lead the group in prayer that Baptists will continue to make major contributions to the cause of Christ and in so doing give God the glory.

Baptists

What Makes a Baptist a Baptist?

The following suggestions for leaders of group study are based on Baptist Identity Leaflet No. 2.

Scripture Memory

"...Always be prepared to give an answer to everyone who asks you to give the reason for the hope that you have. But do this with gentleness and respect...." 1 Peter 3:15 (NIV)

Getting Started

Begin the meeting with prayer. Request the group to read in unison the scripture printed in the Scripture Memory section above that is also printed in the leaflet and in the *Personal Study Guides* book. Lead the group in memorizing the scripture.

Briefly share with the group about J. B. Gambrell and read aloud the quotation by him at the bottom of the first page of the leaflet. [If you are not familiar with his biography, research that prior to the meeting. In summary, he was born in 1841 in South Carolina, enlisted in the Confederate Army, served as a scout in the Army of Northern Virginia commanded by General Robert E. Lee, pastored in Mississippi, was editor of the state Baptist paper in Mississippi, president of Mercer University in Georgia, corresponding secretary (now termed executive director) of the Baptist General Convention of Texas, editor of the *Baptist Standard*, and served as president of the Southern Baptist Convention. He died in Dallas, Texas, in 1921.]

Read aloud the statement at the beginning of the leaflet: "I just believe in being a Christian. I don't want to be part of a denomination." Ask, Why do you think a person might make such a statement? Indicate that this study will help to clarify that such a statement indicates a lack of understanding about what a denomination is.

Guiding the Group Study

Lead a discussion on each of the subsections of the leaflet. Here are some suggested discussion starters, or you may choose to develop your own.

What Is a Denomination? Ask, What is the difference between a "denomination" and a "religious organization"? How are the two related? What are some examples of a denomination and of an organization that is part of a denomination? [Be prepared to give examples in case the members cannot.] Indicate that some persons declare that denominations are no longer viable. Ask, Do you agree or disagree with that? What is the basis of your answer? [Note that the Baptist denomination worldwide has grown in numbers and ministers to millions of persons in numerous ways.]

What Makes Baptists Distinctive? Ask, What are some of the common ideas that persons have about what makes the Baptist denomination distinct from others? What actually makes Baptists a distinct denomination? What are the basic ingredients in the Baptist "recipe" of beliefs, polities, and practices? As these are stated, write them in a format large enough for the group to read.

Why Is There a Lack of Knowledge about Baptists? Ask, What are some factors you have experienced that help to explain why many Baptists are not fully aware of the ingredients in the Baptist Recipe?

The Growing Interest in Baptist Beliefs. Ask, Why do you think that there is an attitude among many persons that denominations are a bad thing rather than good? What evidence do you see, if any, that there is a growing interest among Baptists about Baptist heritage, beliefs, and practices? What can be done to increase such interest? Why is this important? [Be prepared to give answers.] If the size of the group allows, divide it into smaller groups to brainstorm these questions. For each group select a person to moderate the discussion and another to report to the total group the ideas that are mentioned. At the end of a designated time, call the groups together for reports and discussion.

What Difference Does It Make? Ask, What are some of the major contributions the Baptist denomination has made both to individuals and to society as a whole? What do you think is the most important contribution that the Baptist denomination has made?

Closing

Request persons to share with the group what they appreciate most about the Baptist denomination. Ask, How can Baptists tell non-Baptists why they are appreciative of the Baptist denomination without appearing arrogant or antagonistic? Lead the members of the group in reviewing the Fill in the Blanks section and the Application Questions in the *Personal Study Guides* book.

Prayer Time

Lead the group in praying that Baptists will understand the importance of their denomination and that it will continue to make positive contributions in the name of the Lord Jesus Christ.

Jesus Is Lord

The following suggestions for leaders of group study are based on Baptist Identity Leaflet No. 3.

Scripture Memory

*"…every tongue should confess that Jesus Christ is Lord,
to the glory of God the Father."* Philippians 2:11

Getting Started

Begin the meeting with prayer. Request the group to read in unison Philippians 2:11 printed in the Scripture Memory section above as well as in the leaflet and the *Personal Study Guides* book. Lead the group in memorizing the scripture. Indicate that one of the earliest Christian statements of faith was, "Jesus is Lord."

Share that George W. Truett is considered to be historically one of the foremost leaders of Baptists. [If you are not familiar with his biography, research that prior to the meeting. Briefly, he was born in North Carolina in 1867, founded a school in Georgia as a young man, moved to Texas with his family, and after graduating from Baylor University became pastor of the First Baptist Church of Dallas. During his pastorate from 1897 to 1944 the church membership grew tenfold, to almost eight thousand. He served in numerous key positions in Baptist life, including president of the Baptist World Alliance. In 1920 he preached a famous sermon to a crowd of fifteen thousand persons from the east steps of the Capitol in Washington.] In regard to the Lordship of Christ, he made this statement in the sermon:

> That doctrine is for Baptists the dominant fact in all their Christian experience, the nerve center of all their Christian life, the bedrock of all their church polity, the sheet anchor of all their hopes, the climax and crown of all their rejoicings…. From that germinal concept of the absolute Lordship of Christ, all our Baptist principles emerge.

Read the quote aloud. Ask, What are some special emphases that Baptists give to the belief that Jesus is Lord? When a dictator or a ruling group of a country demands that ultimate allegiance be given to the state, what ought the Baptist response be? What are some examples from history or current events of such a demand and how Baptists have responded? [Note: Be prepared to supply these examples in case the group is not able to do so.]

Guiding the Group Study

Lead a discussion on each of the subsections of the leaflet. Here are some suggested discussion starters, or you may choose to develop your own.

The Bible Teaches the Lordship of Christ. In a format large enough for the group to read, list each of the four ways provided in the leaflet that supports the biblical teaching regarding the Lordship of Christ. Request a person to read from the leaflet the scripture passage that relates to each of these four, and then lead a discussion about how these could be part of a presentation of the gospel to someone who is not a Christian.

The Extent of the Lordship of Christ. Ask, What does it mean when we say that Jesus is Lord of all? Request a person to read from the leaflet the scripture passage that relates to each of the three specific ways mentioned in the leaflet regarding Jesus being Lord. Lead a discussion on the meaning of Christ's Lordship in each of these three areas.

The Lordship of Christ and Soul Competency. Ask, What does the term "soul competency" mean? Indicate that this is a term that Baptists have used through the years but it may not communicate well with some people. Ask, How else could the concept be expressed? State that persons have the competency and responsibility to find and follow Christ's will as Lord. Ask, What are some ways that we can do this? [Ideas: Bible study, prayer, worship, Christian fellowship]

The Lordship of Christ Mandates Religious Freedom. Point out that all Christian denominations recognize in some way the Lordship of Christ. Ask, Why were Baptists persecuted by the governments in England and Colonial America in the seventeenth and eighteenth centuries for their expression of this doctrine?

The Lordship of Christ and a New Testament Church Are Inseparable. Ask, What are some ways that the Lordship of Christ is to be applied to each church? Lead a discussion on how the Lordship of Christ can be demonstrated in your church.

Closing

Ask, How does a person's trust in Jesus as Lord affect the life of a church? Of a family? Of a person in his or her daily work? Request members to volunteer to describe how each of the following assists them in finding and following the will of Jesus as Lord of life: prayer, Bible study, worship, and Christian fellowship. Lead the members of the group in reviewing the Fill in the Blanks section and the Application Questions in the *Personal Study Guides* book.

Prayer Time

Request the members to close their eyes and to prayerfully consider the meaning of the Lordship of Christ to them personally. Then conclude with a prayer of commitment to Christ's Lordship.

The Authority of the Bible

The following suggestions for leaders of group study are based on Baptist Identity Leaflet No. 4.

Scripture Memory

*"All Scripture is God-breathed and is useful for teaching,
rebuking, correcting and training in righteousness,
so that the man of God may be thoroughly equipped for every good work."*
2 Timothy 3:16-17 (NIV)

Getting Started

Begin the meeting with prayer. Request the group to read in unison 2 Timothy 3:16-17 printed in the box on the first page of the leaflet as well as in the Scripture Memory section above and in the *Personal Study Guides* book. Lead the group to memorize this scripture.

Request persons to volunteer to share about the first time they remember having their own Bible. Ask, What is one of the most memorable experiences you have had in reading the Bible? When is a time that a memorized scripture passage comforted you or gave you a sense of direction in a decision?

Read the following statement from George W. Truett that is part of his famous address delivered from the steps of the United States Capitol in 1920 to over fifteen thousand persons:

> The Bible and the Bible alone is the rule of faith and practice for Baptists. To them the one standard by which all creeds and conduct and character must be tried is the Word of God. They ask only one question concerning all religious faith and practice, and that question is, "What saith the Word of God?" Not traditions, nor customs, nor councils, nor confessions, nor ecclesiastical formularies, however venerable and pretentious, guide Baptists, but simply and solely the will of Christ as they find it revealed in the New Testament.

Guiding the Group Study

Lead a discussion on each of the subsections of the leaflet. Here are some suggested discussion starters, or you may choose to develop your own.

Baptists Consider the Bible Authoritative. Ask, Why have Baptists contended that the Bible is divine and thus authoritative? What are the evidences of the divine nature of the Bible?

23

The Nature of the Authority of the Bible. Share with the group why it is important to indicate that Baptists believe the Bible to be the "sole ultimate written authority" rather than the "sole ultimate authority." Share also that Baptists believe that there is no other ultimate "non-written" authority than God—no person or group of persons has that distinction. Ask, Do you agree with Herschel Hobbs' statement about the nature of the Bible that is quoted in the leaflet? Why or why not?

The Authority of the Bible Relates to Other Basic Baptist Beliefs. Emphasize that all of the doctrines and polities of Baptists are based on the Bible and that some of these basic beliefs also relate in special ways to the reading and interpretation of the Bible itself. Lead a discussion on how the Baptist beliefs in soul competency, the priesthood of believers, and religious freedom relate to the use of the Bible. [Note: You may find it helpful to read the leaflets on these particular topics prior to leading these discussions.]

Interpreting the Bible's Teachings. Ask, Why do Baptists believe that all believers should be free to interpret the Bible for themselves rather than having some person or group determine what an official interpretation should be? What are some responsibilities that this freedom places on the believer? What are some basic principles for interpreting the Bible? [Be prepared to discuss these with the group.]

> Case Study. A person who is not a Baptist visits an adult Sunday School class and remarks: "This is not my first time to visit a Baptist Sunday School, and I have been curious about the fact that the teachers have had different backgrounds with no particular level of education in common. Only one teacher had seminary education in the interpretation and teaching of the Bible. Can just anyone teach an adult class in a Baptist church?" Ask, What would be your reply to the person in light of Baptist beliefs?

Closing

Guide a summary discussion on why Baptists have contended that no other document should ever be allowed to replace the Bible as the sole written authority for the Christian faith and practice of individuals and churches. Lead the members of the group in reviewing the Fill in the Blanks section and the Application Questions in the *Personal Study Guides* book.

Prayer Time

Encourage the members to silently reflect on times the Bible was especially meaningful to them. Lead the group in prayer that persons will exercise the freedom we enjoy in our nation to read, interpret, and apply the teachings of the Bible.

Is Soul Competency
THE Baptist Distinctive?

The following suggestions for leaders of group study are based on Baptist Identity Leaflet No. 5.

Scripture Memory

"Choose you this day whom ye will serve."
Joshua 24:15

Getting Started

Begin the meeting with prayer. Lead the group in memorizing the scripture printed in the Scripture Memory section above that is also printed on the first page of the leaflet and in the *Personal Study Guides* book.

Request the group to read in unison the quotes from the three boxes on the front page of the leaflet. State that the concept of soul competency is obviously an important one for Baptists, but the term "soul competency" is not often used in everyday speech and the concept may not be widely understood. Hopefully, this session will aid in both the understanding of and appreciation for the concept of soul competency.

Indicate that one of the quotes in the leaflet is from Herschel Hobbs and that he was one of Baptists most influential pastor/theologians during the latter part of the twentieth century. He often stressed the significance of soul competency. In the book *The Baptist Faith and Message: Revised Edition*, Hobbs wrote about the principle of soul competency in religion: "Out of this principle flow all other elements of Baptist belief such as belief in God in His triune revelation, authority of the Scriptures, baptism, regenerated church membership, local church autonomy, priesthood of believers, social action (both corporate and individual), soul freedom, and the separation of church and state."

Concerning Baptists, Hobbs stated that they "insist that every man shall be free to decide for himself in matters of religion." He added, "This does not mean that Baptists believe that one can believe just anything and be a Christian or a Baptist. The competency of the soul in religion entails the authority of the Scriptures and the lordship of Jesus Christ."

Read to the group the above statements by Hobbs. Ask, Do you agree or disagree that soul competency is the primary Baptist distinctive? What is the basis of your answer?

Guiding the Group Study

Lead a discussion on each of the subsections of the leaflet. Here are some suggested discussion starters, or you may choose to develop your own.

The Meaning of Soul Competency. Request members of the group to share what to them is the basic meaning of soul competency. Ask, In what way is this not a "mere human characteristic, but a gift from God"? Why do you think that E. Y. Mullins used the words "in religion" in his statement printed in the leaflet about soul competency being a "distinctive Baptist contribution to the world's thought"?

The Bible and Soul Competency. Ask, What are examples of soul competency found in the Old Testament and in the New Testament? Jesus declared that he had "all power" (Matthew 28:18), so why did he not force persons to follow him?

Attacks on and Defense of Soul Competency. Using some method that can easily be viewed by the whole group, make three columns headed: "Limits God's Sovereignty," "Leads to Arrogance," and "Results in Subjectivism." Lead a discussion on appropriate answers to these criticisms of the concept of soul competency and make notes in each column summarizing the discussion. Ask, What is the relation of soul competency to both freedom and responsibility in the Christian life?

Soul Competency and Other Baptist Beliefs. Ask, How does soul competency relate to the belief of Baptists in the authority of the Bible, in religious freedom, in the priesthood of all believers, and in believer's baptism? If the size of the group is such that it can be divided into four subgroups, divide it and give each group an assignment to discuss the relation of soul competency to one of these beliefs. For each group select a person to moderate the discussion and another to report a summary of the group's discussion when the total group reconvenes. Set a time limit for the small group discussions, and at the end of the time call the groups together for the sharing of the reports.

Closing

Ask, Was the term soul competency a familiar one to you before this session? What other terms do you believe would also communicate the concept of soul competency? How do you apply soul competency in your daily life? Your family? Your church? Lead the members of the group in reviewing the Fill in the Blanks section and the Application Questions in the *Personal Study Guides* book.

Prayer Time

Lead the group to prayerfully reflect on both the opportunities and responsibilities that accompany soul competency.

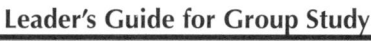

Baptists:
Salvation By Grace Through Faith Alone

The following suggestions for leaders of group study are based on Baptist Identity Leaflet No. 6.

Scripture Memory

"For by grace are ye saved through faith; and that not of yourselves: it is the gift of God: Not of works, lest any man should boast."
Ephesians 2:8-9

Getting Started

Begin the meeting with prayer. Request the group to read in unison the scripture printed in the Scripture Memory section above that is also printed on the first page of the leaflet and in the *Personal Study Guides* book. Lead the group to memorize the scripture.

Request volunteers to share ways they have encountered of how some persons feel they can get to heaven apart from faith in Jesus Christ. [You might consider giving illustrations from cartoons, television, movies, or books that indicate persons entering heaven based on good works with no mention of faith in Christ.] Ask, What are some of the works-based approaches to salvation common in the world in both religious and secular thought? Why is the concept of salvation based on ritual or good works widely accepted?

Read aloud the quotation in the box in the center of the leaflet. Indicate that one of the most challenging questions in regard to the Bible's teaching about salvation is, "What is the relation of God's sovereignty and human freedom of choice?" Indicate that the answer Herschel Hobbs gives in the quote is one way that Baptists have answered the question. Inquire if the members of the group can think of other answers that have been or could be given.

Guiding the Group Study

Lead a discussion on each of the subsections of the leaflet. Here are some suggested discussion starters, or you may choose to develop your own.

Grace/Faith Alone for Salvation. Describe the biblical concept of faith. Ask, How does the Bible present the relationship of faith and grace in regard to salvation? Why are the two terms closely related? How does the Bible present the relationship of faith and works in Ephesians 2:8-10?

Salvation Is Both Free and Costly. Ask, How is salvation in Christ both free and costly? What did it cost God to provide our salvation? What did it cost Jesus?

Salvation Is a Process of Grace through Faith. Ask, What is the biblical basis for speaking of salvation in Christ as a process and not just a onetime response to God's grace? What are the three stages or phases of this process found most often in Baptist statements of faith? As these are stated, write them in a format large enough for the group to read. Lead a discussion on each one of these.

True Faith Cannot Be Forced. Ask, How is the fact that true faith cannot be forced related to the strong and historic Baptist emphasis on religious freedom? Ask, What are some possible ways that the gospel can be shared with an unsaved person that avoid coercion?

Grace/Faith and God's Sovereignty/Humankind's Free Will. Read aloud the following quotation from Herschel Hobbs' book *The Baptist Faith and Message: Revised Edition*: "Obviously, to finite intellects, it is impossible to harmonize God's sovereignty and man's free will. But in the infinite wisdom of God there is no conflict (Rom. 11:33-36)." Ask, Why is there an apparent contradiction in the belief in God's sovereignty and in the belief in the free will of human beings? How can a proper understanding of grace and faith point to a way to show that the two beliefs are not contradictory? What is the relationship of "faith" and "repentance"?

Closing

Summarize the works approach to salvation. Ask, How does this differ from the grace/faith emphasis of Baptists? What are some of the misconceptions that people have of a grace/faith only approach to salvation? How can we avoid these in our own thinking? Lead the members of the group in reviewing the Fill in the Blanks section and the Application Questions in the *Personal Study Guides* book.

Prayer Time

Indicate that grace involves the unmerited love of God for lost persons that makes salvation possible. Request the group to sing or read in unison the words to the hymn "Amazing Grace." If a hymnal with the words to "Amazing Grace" is not available for the group to use, print the words in advance and have copies for each member. If possible, have a recording of the hymn to play during a silent prayer time in which the members are asked to pray thanking God for the grace gift of salvation in Jesus Christ. Urge anyone in the group who has not accepted Christ as Lord and Savior to do so.

Baptists:

The Priesthood of the *Believer* or of *Believers?*

The following suggestions for leaders of group study are based on Baptist Identity Leaflet No. 7.

Scripture Memory

"Ye are a chosen generation, a royal priesthood, a holy nation, a peculiar people; that ye should shew forth the praises of him who hath called you out of darkness into his marvelous light." 1 Peter 2:9

Getting Started

Begin the meeting with prayer. Request the group to read in unison the scripture printed in the Scripture Memory section above that is also printed inside the leaflet under the Bibles and in the *Personal Study Guides* book. Lead the group in memorizing the scripture (1 Peter 2:9).

Read aloud the quote in the box on the front of the leaflet and then write in a format large enough for the group to read these three phrases: "The Priesthood of THE Believer," "The Priesthood of BELIEVERS," and "The Priesthood of ALL Believers." [Note: Write the words "THE," "BELIEVERS," and "ALL" in capital letters.] Indicate that these three phrases relate to different, although similar, aspects of this basic Baptist belief. Baptists may not all agree on the exact meaning of the concept of the priesthood of believers, but it is one of the most treasured doctrines for Baptists.

Guiding the Group Study

Lead a discussion on each of the subsections of the leaflet. Here are some suggested discussion starters, or you may choose to develop your own.

What Does It Mean to Be a Priest? Ask, What role did priests have in the Old Testament? In what ways did Jesus replace the High Priest of the Old Testament? What are the opportunities of priesthood? The responsibilities?

Where Did the Concept of the Priesthood of Believers Come From? Give a brief account of the Protestant Reformation. Indicate that although Baptists hold many beliefs in common with the leaders of the Reformation, they also hold several views that are very different; persons who held Baptist beliefs were persecuted by the Reformers. Ask, Why do Baptists trace their view of the priesthood of "believers" to the New Testament instead of to the Reformation?

The Priesthood of The Believer. Ask, In what way is the concept of the priesthood of "the believer" related to that of soul competency? What are some of the responsibilities of a believer priest as a member of a church?

In light of the fact that all members of a church are to be believer priests with soul competency and direct access to God without need of a human mediator, what is the role of a pastor to be? What are some of the responsibilities of a pastor?

The Priesthood of Believers. Ask, In what way is the emphasis on the plural "believers" important to the Baptist concept of what a church is to be? Baptists are sometimes accused of focusing on the individual or personal aspect of the Christian faith to the neglect of the group or community aspect. Ask, How does an understanding of the priesthood of believers help to provide a balance?

Challenges to the Priesthood of All Believers. Ask, What are some of the main challenges to the concept of the priesthood of all believers? What responses can be made to these?

> Case Study. A pastorless Baptist church in seeking a pastor elects a pastor search committee by participation of the members of the church. The committee after months of prayerful searching recommends a person to be the pastor. The church members vote to call the person to be the pastor, and the person accepts. A few Sundays later in a sermon the new pastor announces that God speaks to the church through him and that he is the authority for determining what the Bible teaches about how the church is to function. In light of the biblical teaching of the priesthood of all believers, what do you believe the response of the church members should be?

Closing

Ask, What are some new insights about the positive benefits or opportunities of being a believer priest that you have gained from this study? What are some of the awesome responsibilities? Lead the members of the group in reviewing the Fill in the Blanks section and the Application Questions in the *Personal Study Guides* book.

Prayer Time

Request the members to prayerfully reflect on the opportunities and responsibilities of being believer priests. Then lead a closing prayer of commitment to be faithful to this biblical teaching.

Baptists:
Believer's Baptism

The following suggestions for leaders of group study are based on Baptist Identity Leaflet No. 8.

Scripture Memory

"Therefore we are buried with him by baptism into death:
that like as Christ was raised up from the dead by the glory of the Father,
even so we also should walk in newness of life." Romans 6:4

Getting Started

Begin the meeting with prayer. Indicate that one of the most distinguishing characteristics of Baptists is the belief in believer's baptism by immersion, although at one time some Baptists sprinkled or poured water on the person being baptized. Careful study of the Bible eventually led Baptists in the early 1600s to view immersion as the biblical method. There were difficulties associated with the practice of immersion. For example, baptisms were performed outside in rivers and lakes; there were no baptisteries inside church buildings. Often non-Baptists gathered to watch and to ridicule those participating in the baptism. The terms "baptizers" and "baptists" at first were terms of mockery. In spite of the difficulties, immersion became the standard Baptist practice, and eventually the "baptizers" accepted the name that had been hurled at them in ridicule. Thus, the statement on baptism from the 1644 First London Confession that is printed in the leaflet is of special importance in Baptist heritage; request someone to read the statement.

Request the group to read in unison the scripture in the Scripture Memory section above that is also printed in the center of the leaflet and in the *Personal Study Guides* book. Lead the group to memorize the scripture.

Guiding the Group Study

Lead a discussion on each of the subsections of the leaflet. Here are some suggested discussion starters, or you may choose to develop your own.

Baptism Is Only for Believers. Ask, Why do many people think that believer's baptism by immersion is the primary Baptist distinctive? How would you respond to someone who expresses this viewpoint? What is the basis for the refusal of Baptists to baptize infants? Why in the New Testament did baptism always follow conversion and did not precede it?

Baptism Is Only by Immersion. Ask, What are some of the reasons that persons may be reluctant to be baptized by immersion? [Hint: Some adults who have truly believed in Christ as their Lord and Savior may have never been baptized by immersion as a believer, and they may feel that baptism is unnecessary because it is not essential for salvation. Those who experienced infant baptism may feel that another baptism is not significant. Some may wonder why baptism is important since it is symbolic and not sacramental. Others may feel unworthy, and some may fear immersion.] Lead a discussion on the five reasons mentioned in the leaflet for the Baptist belief in baptism only by immersion.

Baptism Is Symbolic. Ask, What are some of the things that immersion symbolizes? As these are stated, write them in a format large enough for the group to read.

> Case Study. Sam Houston was the commanding general in the Texas army in the Texas Revolution of 1836, the first elected president of the Republic of Texas, and a senator from Texas after Texas became part of the United States of America. During his term as senator he made a public profession of faith in Christ in 1854 at the Independence Baptist Church in Independence, Texas, and was baptized by immersion in a nearby creek. Someone is reported to have said, "Well, senator, I hear your sins have been washed away in the water." Houston supposedly replied in jest, "If so, then God help the fish downstream!" Whether or not the account of his statement is true, it illustrates a false idea held by some that baptism washes away sin. Ask, What would you say to counter this idea and explain the real purpose of baptism?

Person, Place, Timing, and Setting for Baptisms. Ask, Why do Baptists have public rather than private baptismal services? What length of time do you think should exist between a person's public profession of faith in Christ and his or her baptism? Why? Indicate that Baptists have no denominationally prescribed practices in regard to baptisms, such as when they are performed, where, by whom, and what is said by the person who conducts the baptism during the baptism itself. Ask, What are the practices of your church in these matters?

Closing

Request persons to volunteer descriptions of baptismal services they have observed in various Baptist churches and indicate what features of the service they found especially inspirational. Encourage anyone in the group who is a believer in Christ but has not experienced believer's baptism to do so. Lead the members of the group in reviewing the Fill in the Blanks section and the Application Questions in the *Personal Study Guides* book.

Prayer Time

Lead in prayer that baptismal services will truly be worship experiences and that persons being baptized and those in the congregation will reflect on the meaning to them personally of this beautiful, symbolic expression of life in Christ and obedience to his command.

Baptists Believe in a Regenerate Church Membership

The following suggestions for leaders of group study are based on Baptist Identity Leaflet No. 9.

Scripture Memory

"And the Lord added to the church daily such as should be saved."
Acts 2:47

Getting Started

Begin the meeting with prayer. Point out that a number of passages in the New Testament indicate that a church is to be made up only of persons who have responded to God's grace gift of salvation through faith in Jesus Christ. One of those is the passage printed on the first page of the leaflet (Acts 2:47) as well as in the Scripture Memory section above and in the *Personal Study Guides* book. Request the group to read the passage in unison and then lead the members to memorize it.

Request each person to write his or her definition of "church" and to volunteer to share the definition with the group. Then lead a discussion about how what each has written relates to the definition in the introductory statement of the leaflet. Ask, What other term or terms do you think would convey the concept of regenerate?

Guiding the Group Study

Lead a discussion on each of the subsections of the leaflet. Here are some suggested discussion starters, or you may choose to develop your own.

Why Should Only Believers in Christ Be Members of a Church? Ask, Why are both of the following statements important: "Only believers in Christ should be members of a church" and "Believers in Christ ought to be members of a church"? What is the biblical basis for each statement?

How Do Persons Become Members of a Baptist Church? Ask, What are the policies of your church in regard to a person seeking membership who has never been a member of any church? What is the policy in regard to a person who is already a member of a Baptist church? What is the policy in regard to a person who is a member of a church other than Baptist? [Note: If you are not familiar with the policies, obtain this information prior to the meeting.] If your church does not have a policy on these matters, what would be the process of developing one?

Is There Evidence of a Decline in Regenerate Church Membership? Request the group to read in unison the statement by William R. Estep in the box in the center of the leaflet. Ask, Do you agree or disagree with the evidence mentioned in the leaflet of a decline in a regenerate church membership? Why? Have you noted any of these in your church?

What Has Caused the Erosion of the Ideal of Regenerate Church Membership? Ask, Which of the factors mentioned in the leaflet have you been aware of? Which do you think are the most serious threats to the ideal of a regenerate church membership?

Should a Decline in a Regenerate Church Membership Be a Concern? Ask, Do you agree with the reasons set forth in the leaflet why a decline should be a concern? If you agree, why do you? If you do not agree, why don't you? What other reasons would you add?

What Can Be Done to More Thoroughly Achieve a Regenerate Church Membership? Describe the process of your church for attempting to discern whether a person seeking membership has been truly born again. If your church does not have such a process, discuss how one might be developed. Ask, What are some possible dangers inherent in such a process? If persons in the group have been through a class for new church members, ask them to describe the class and their impression of it.

Closing

Ask, What is the relation of a regenerate church membership to the New Testament ideal of the love the members are to have for one another? Lead the members of the group in reviewing the Fill in the Blanks section and the Application Questions in the *Personal Study Guides* book.

Prayer Time

Request members of the group to pray silently for these matters: that their church will be concerned about maintaining a regenerate church membership, that the policies and practices of their church in regard to new members will be constructive, and that opportunity will be given for each person seeking membership to consider whether or not he or she has had a genuine experience of faith in Jesus Christ as Lord and Savior.

Congregational Church Governance

The following suggestions for leaders of group study are based on Baptist Identity Leaflet No. 10.

Scripture Memory

"So in Christ we who are many form one body, and each member belongs to all the others." Romans 12:5 (NIV)

Getting Started

Begin the meeting with prayer. Request the group to read in unison the scripture printed in the center of the leaflet that is also printed in the Scripture Memory section above and in the *Personal Study Guides* book. Lead the members of the group to memorize the passage of scripture.

In a format large enough for the group to read, make two columns, one labeled "Bases for Congregational Church Governance" and the other "Challenges to Congregational Church Governance." Indicate that governance of the church by the members sets Baptists apart from many other denominations and that it is one of the most challenging of the Baptist polities to maintain.

Request someone to describe the decision process in your church for determining what the church's budget will be, or what changes if any need to be made to the church's facilities, or who will be called to be pastor of the church. Indicate that this process is part of congregational governance. [Note: If you do not know what the process is, find out before the meeting.]

Guiding the Group Study

Lead a discussion on each of the subsections of the leaflet. Here are some suggested discussion starters, or you may choose to develop your own.

What Is Congregational Church Governance? Ask, What does "congregational" mean? What does "polity" mean? Why is the way that a church is governed a part of the church's polity?

What Are the Bases for Congregational Church Governance? Using what has been previously prepared, under the column labeled "Bases for Congregational Church Governance," list the following: The Lordship of Christ, The Authority of the Bible, Salvation Only by Grace through Faith, Soul Competency and the Priesthood of Believers, and Regenerate Church Membership of Baptized Believers. Based on the leaflet, lead a discussion on how each of these is foundational to congregational church governance.

Questions and Issues. Indicate that the word "democracy" means rule by the people. Ask, Why is it not entirely accurate to describe the form of Baptist church governance as a democracy? Ask, What would be some other terms to use to describe Baptist church governance? Ask, What is the appropriate role for a pastor and for deacons in Baptist church governance? It may not be feasible for all decisions in a church to be made by all of the people. Ask, What is a way for all the church members to be ultimately involved in church governance under Christ's Lordship?

Some Factors Undermining Congregational Church Governance. Under the column previously prepared labeled "Challenges to Congregational Church Governance," list the factors that are mentioned in the leaflet as undermining such governance: unsaved church members, immature Christian church members, apathy and indifference in church members, efforts of a person or group in the church to dominate, lack of knowledge about Baptist beliefs and polity. Lead a discussion on how each of these could be dealt with in a constructive, positive way.

Why Congregational Church Governance Is Important. Ask, In what ways does congregational church governance contribute to the development of Christian maturity in the members and to the vitality of a church?

Ways to Strengthen Congregational Church Governance. Read aloud each of the ways mentioned in the leaflet. Ask, How can, or does, your church carry these out?

Closing

Request the members of the group to share ways that they have experienced congregational governance functioning in churches where they have been members. Encourage the group to participate in the governance of their church. Lead the members of the group in reviewing the Fill in the Blanks section and the Application Questions in the *Personal Study Guides* book.

Prayer Time

Lead the group in prayer that their church will gain vitality and maturity through congregational church governance.

Baptist Autonomy:
Difficulties and Benefits

The following suggestions for leaders of group study are based on Baptist Identity Leaflet No. 11.

Scripture Memory

"I am Alpha and Omega, the first and the last: and, What thou seest, write in a book, and send it unto the seven churches which are in Asia."
Revelation 1:11

Getting Started

Begin the meeting with prayer. Explain that the first association of churches in Texas was established in 1840 by Baptists who had come to Texas, which was then an independent republic, from many different places. Although they differed in some ways as to beliefs and practices, they were committed to the autonomy of each Baptist church and wrote that commitment into the founding documents of the association. The statement printed in the box on the front of the leaflet is an example of Baptist commitment to autonomy. Request the group to read the statement in unison. [Note: Be prepared to define "ecclesiastical."]

Then request the group to read in unison the scripture found in the box in the center of the leaflet (Revelation 1:11) that is also printed in the Scripture Memory section above and in the *Personal Study Guides* book. Lead the group in memorizing this scripture.

Guiding the Group Study

Lead a discussion on each of the subsections of the leaflet. Here are some suggested discussion starters, or you may choose to develop your own.

The Meaning of Autonomy of Baptist Churches. Many denominations use the term "Church" to refer to the denomination, such as the Roman Catholic Church. Ask, Why is it incorrect to use the term "The Baptist Church" when referring to the Baptist denomination? What are some of the practices of a Baptist church that indicate it is autonomous? As these are mentioned, write them in a format large enough for the group to read. Lead a discussion on each of these about how your church can maintain or strengthen these practices.

The Biblical Basis for Church Autonomy. Ask, Why is it important for Baptists to base their conviction about church autonomy on the Bible? What are some examples in the New Testament of church autonomy? What is the relation of congregational church governance and church autonomy? Of religious freedom and church autonomy?

Some Misconceptions about Baptist Autonomy. Ask, Why is it incorrect to speak of "levels" in Baptist denominational organization, such as the "associational level," the "state convention level," and the "national convention level"? Ask, Since these various parts of Baptist organizational life have no authority over other parts, how can they work together to advance the causes of Christ?

Some Possible Threats to Baptist Autonomy. In a format large enough for the members of the group to read, make two columns, one headed "Threats from Outside" and the other headed "Threats from Within." Ask, What are some of the threats to Baptist church freedom from outside of a church? From within a church? List each as it is mentioned. Lead a discussion on ways to counter each of these.

> Case Study. A Baptist convention adopts a statement of faith as its official statement. During a business meeting of a local church, a member of the congregation who has recently joined from another denomination asks why the church is not required to adopt this same statement of faith since the church cooperates with the convention. Ask, What would be an appropriate response to this question?

Some Difficulties Related to Baptist Autonomy. Ask, What are some of the challenges or difficulties associated with local church autonomy? How does your church strive to overcome these?

The Benefits of Baptist Autonomy. Ask, Do you believe that the benefits of autonomy outweigh the difficulties associated with it? Why or why not? Which benefits do you believe are most important?

Closing

Ask, How do Baptists endeavor to avoid either total independence of congregations or complete submission of congregations to outside authorities? Lead the members of the group in reviewing the Fill in the Blanks section and the Application Questions in the *Personal Study Guides* book.

Prayer Time

Lead in prayer for your church to be effective in fulfilling the Great Commission and the Great Commandment while also maintaining its autonomy.

Baptist Church Life:
Organization, Officers, Worship, Ordinances

The following suggestions for leaders of group study are based on Baptist Identity Leaflet No. 12.

Scripture Memory

"…speaking the truth in love, we will in all things grow up into him who is the Head, that is, Christ. From him the whole body, joined and held together by every supporting ligament, grows and builds itself up in love, as each part does its work." Ephesians 4:15-16 (NIV)

Getting Started

Begin the meeting with prayer. Request the group to read in unison Ephesians 4:15-16 printed in the Scripture Memory section above, in the box in the center of the leaflet, and in the *Personal Study Guides* book. Lead the group to memorize this passage. Then read aloud the quote by William R. Estep on the first page of the leaflet and indicate that hopefully this study will assist in understanding how the emphasis on freedom relates to areas of church life in addition to worship.

Ask, What is the relationship of the Baptist emphasis on local church autonomy and the emphasis on freedom in Baptist church life? Indicate that Baptist churches differ in a number of ways from one another, but they have many things in common. Request the members to name some of the things that Baptist churches have in common, and as they do so, write them in a format large enough for the group to read. [Hint: selects its own pastoral leadership, the Lord's Supper as symbolic, baptism of believers only and only by immersion, worship services that include Bible reading, preaching, prayer, and singing]

Guiding the Group Study

Lead a discussion on each of the subsections of the leaflet. Here are some suggested discussion starters, or you may choose to develop your own.

Church Organization. Indicate that although the Bible has few specifics about the organization of a church, the Bible does set forth the basic nature and function of a church. Ask, What are some of these? [Hint: worship, evangelism, discipleship of believers, Christian education, missions, ministry, and fellowship] Ask, What are some examples of how a church's organization relates to a function such as evangelism, Bible Study, Christian education, or worship? [Hint: The organization for Sunday School in a church relates to evangelism and to Christian education.]

Worship. Request the members to share with the group how the various aspects of worship in their church are personally meaningful to them, such as Bible reading, praying, singing, preaching, and gathering of tithes and offerings. Ask, In what ways do the attitudes and preparation of the worshippers contribute to the effectiveness of worship services?

> Case Study. The membership in a Baptist church is divided over what kind of worship service the church should have on Sunday morning. Some want a very formal, structured worship, and others want a very informal, unstructured worship. Feelings are strong, and the possibility of a split in the church is growing. Ask, What do you suggest should be done?

Church Officers. Ask, What is the process in your church for the selection of a pastor? Of deacons? What comment about the process do you have, if any? What do you find the most meaningful aspect of the ordination services in your church to be? What, if anything, do you believe could be done to make ordination services even more meaningful?

Church Ordinances. Read the scriptures referenced in the leaflet that apply to baptism and the Lord's Supper. Ask, Why are these two ordinances important even though they are not necessary for salvation? How do congregational governance and the Lordship of Christ relate to the two ordinances? Indicate that unleavened bread and the fruit of the vine were the symbols Jesus used to portray his death. Most of the time these elements are the symbols used in a Baptist church. Ask, Why do you think that these are the elements most commonly used?

Closing

Indicate that total freedom in church organization, worship, and activities would result in anarchy and ineffectiveness. On the other hand, dictatorial control by one person or by a small group violates basic biblical guidelines for church life. Ask, How does your church utilize freedom to provide effective organization, worship, and activities? Lead the members of the group in reviewing the Fill in the Blanks section and the Application Questions in the *Personal Study Guides* book.

Prayer Time

Ask the members to pray silently for a spirit of unity in the life of their church.

Baptists and Voluntary Cooperation

The following suggestions for leaders of group study are based on Baptist Identity Leaflet No. 13.

Scripture Memory

"Entirely on their own, they urgently pleaded with us for the privilege of sharing in this service to the saints." 2 Corinthians 8:3-4 (NIV)

Getting Started

Begin the meeting with prayer. Request the group to read in unison 2 Corinthians 8:3-4 printed in the Scripture Memory section above and also at the top of the leaflet and in the *Personal Study Guides* book. Lead them to memorize this passage.

Ask, Why did early Baptists consider that the autonomy of churches and the command of Jesus to take the gospel to the entire world presented a dilemma?

Guiding the Group Study

Lead a discussion on each of the subsections of the leaflet. Here are some suggested discussion starters, or you may choose to develop your own.

The Bases for VOLUNTARY Cooperation. Using the leaflet as a resource, in a format large enough for the group to read, list the Baptist beliefs that are the bases for voluntary cooperation. In advance of the meeting, print out the scripture passages that are referenced for each of the six bases for voluntary cooperation on a separate card or piece of paper for each scripture. Distribute these at the meeting and request the members to read these aloud one at a time after you read the statement in the leaflet that relates to each. Ask, What other bases can you think of for voluntary cooperation related to Baptist beliefs?

The Bases for Voluntary COOPERATION. Ask, In what ways do the scriptures cited in the leaflet support the concept of voluntary cooperation? What other examples in the New Testament do you think of that support this view?

The Nature of VOLUNTARY COOPERATION. Request the members to name specific examples of each of the approaches to voluntary cooperation found in the Baptist denomination. [Be prepared to give examples if the members cannot think of any, such as the name of the Baptist association of churches of which your church is part, the name of the Baptist state or regional organization to which your church relates, or the name of one or more national Baptist organizations to which your church relates.] Request members to share any experiences they have had personally with one or more of these, such as attending meetings, serving as an elected officer, or being on a committee.

The Benefits of Voluntary Cooperation. Ask, How does voluntary cooperation benefit churches? Individual Baptists? Baptist institutions? The cause of Christ? What are some specific examples of each of these? In what ways is your church involved in Baptist voluntary cooperation? [Note: If you and/or the members of the group are not knowledgeable about Baptist denominational cooperation, you might ask your pastor or a church staff member for information.]

Responses to the Challenges to Denominational Voluntary Cooperation. Ask, How valid do you believe the challenges and/or criticisms mentioned in the leaflet to be? Why? How valid do you believe each of the responses to these challenges and/or criticisms to be? Why? Which one or ones do you believe to be the most convincing as to why persons and churches should support voluntary cooperation?

> Case Study. A member of a denomination that has an hierarchical approach to organization says, "Freedom is a wonderful thing, but you Baptists take it to extreme. Your approach is inefficient at best and leads to anarchy at worst. The Baptist denomination has no control over who your church's pastor will be, how internal church disputes will be settled, what your church contributes to denominational missions, or really anything." Ask, What would your response be in light of the Baptist belief in voluntary cooperation?

Closing

Request the group to read in unison the quote by James L. Sullivan from *Rope of Sand with Strength of Steel.* Ask, Do you believe that the material in the leaflet helps to substantiate this imagery of Baptist life? If so, why? If not, why not? Lead the members of the group in reviewing the Fill in the Blanks section and the Application Questions in the *Personal Study Guides* book.

Prayer Time

Briefly review the benefits and challenges to voluntary cooperation. Request the members to pray silently that nothing will stand in the way of Baptists working together to advance the cause of Christ.

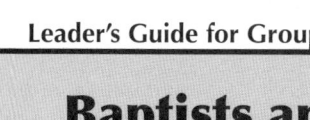

Baptists and Evangelism

The following suggestions for leaders of group study are based on Baptist Identity Leaflet No. 14.

Scripture Memory

*"So then faith cometh by hearing,
and hearing by the word of God."* Romans 10:17

Getting Started

Begin the meeting with prayer. Enlist a person to lead the group in a unison reading of Romans 10:17 found in the center of the leaflet as well as in the Scripture Memory section above and in the *Personal Study Guides* book. Enlist another person to lead the group in a unison reading of the quote from *The Watchman* in the box at the top of the leaflet. After the group has read these in unison, request someone to quote or read John 3:16. Lead the group in memorizing Romans 10:17.

Ask, Do you agree with the statement that "commitment to evangelism as a priority is evident in practically every aspect of Baptist life"? What is the basis of your response?

Guiding the Group Study

Lead a discussion on each of the subsections of the leaflet. Here are some suggested discussion starters, or you may choose to develop your own.

The Bases of Evangelism. Request members to volunteer to describe how basic Baptist beliefs are foundational for evangelism, such as the Lordship of Christ, the authority of the Bible, and the nature of salvation. Ask, Since these are such basic beliefs for Baptists, why do you think many Baptists fail to share the gospel with others?

The Means of Evangelism. Request volunteers to share his or her own experience of being evangelized, that is when and how they came to believe in Jesus Christ as their Lord and Savior. The leaflet describes some legitimate or appropriate means or methods of evangelism. Ask, What would be some illegitimate or inappropriate methods? Which evangelistic methods mentioned in the leaflet do you believe are the most important or effective?

Jesus said that his disciples are to be "witnesses unto me" (Acts 1:8). Ask, How does the role of a witness in a courtroom trial indicate something of a disciple's responsibility as a witness unto Christ? [Hint: A witness is not to judge or to argue the case, that is what the judge and lawyers are for.

43

A witness is to truthfully tell what he or she has personally experienced. So it is with a witness for Christ.]

Obstacles and Challenges to Evangelism. Ask, What obstacles or challenges to evangelism would you add to those mentioned in the leaflet? Which of those mentioned do you believe are most often encountered? How do you suggest that these obstacles can be overcome? How can you affirm both the sovereignty of God and the free choice of persons in a way to advance and not impede evangelism?

> Case Study. In a discussion among church members about evangelism, a person says, "I am not comfortable talking to other people about becoming a Christian. I believe that my responsibility in evangelism is to live the very best Christian life that I can. I had rather see a sermon any day than hear one." Ask, What would be an appropriate response to this statement? What is the relation of words and deeds in evangelistic effort?

[Note: This is a very common outlook and deserves a careful discussion. There is no doubt that living an exemplary Christian life aids evangelism. However, the Bible teaches that saving faith in Christ comes by hearing the word of God (Romans 10:17). For a person to be saved, certain facts about Jesus must be known and believed. It is not possible simply by living an exemplary Christian life, as important as that is, to share about Jesus' love for us, that he was sinless and died on the cross for our sins, and that he rose from the dead. Words, printed or spoken, are necessary in order to share the facts of the gospel. Evangelism, that is sharing the Good News, requires words, such as a simple sharing of faith in and facts about Jesus. Of course, knowing the facts is not adequate for salvation. A person needs also to repent of sin and believe in Christ as Savior and Lord.]

Closing

Ask, Do you think that your church is effective in evangelism? Lead a discussion on how your church could be even more effective than it is. Lead the members of the group in reviewing the Fill in the Blanks section and the Application Questions in the *Personal Study Guides* book.

Prayer Time

Request the members to pray silently for each of the three items listed in the conclusion of the leaflet that the Bible teaches are important in order for evangelism to be widespread and effective.

Baptists and Missions

The following suggestions for leaders of group study are based on Baptist Identity Leaflet No. 15.

Scripture Memory

*"Go ye therefore, and teach all nations,
baptizing them in the name of the Father, and of the Son,
and of the Holy Ghost: Teaching them to observe all things whatsoever I
have commanded you."* Matthew 28:19-20

Getting Started

Request the group to read in unison the scripture at the top of the first page of the leaflet (Matthew 28:19-20) that is also printed in the Scripture Memory section above and in the *Personal Study Guides* book. Lead the group in memorizing the scripture passage.

Read aloud the quote by H. E. Dana found in the center of the leaflet and indicate that this session focuses on missions. Missions is one of the most important, inspiring, and yet historically controversial aspects of Baptist life.

Ask, In what ways is the term "mission" used other than Christian missions (such as a military mission or a diplomatic mission) and what do the activities have in common? What is the distinction of what usually is referred to as Christian missions? [Hint: All types of missions involve being sent or going from one place to another, but Christian missions involves being sent by God to share the Good News about Christ.] What is the relationship of evangelism and missions? [Hint: Evangelism is sharing the Good News wherever we are. Christian missions involves being sent or going to another place or setting to share the Good News.] Indicate that in a sense all Christians are "on mission" but that some persons are called and gifted by God for specific mission efforts.

Guiding the Group Study

Lead a discussion on each of the subsections of the leaflet. Here are some suggested discussion starters, or you may choose to develop your own.

The Background of Baptist Missions. Describe the key events in the development of Baptist missionary activity. Ask, Why do you think it took Baptists so long to develop a worldwide missionary effort?

Bases for Missions. Ask, How do two of Baptists' basic beliefs, that is the Lordship of Christ and the authority of the Bible for faith and practice, relate to missions?

Types of Missionary Activity. Ask, In what ways has the concept of missions changed through the years? What are some of the factors that have caused this changing concept? What missions activities is your church involved in? Request members of the group who have been involved in missions activities to briefly share their experiences.

Support for Missions. Ask, What are some of the ways that Baptists support missions? How does the Baptist emphasis on voluntarism relate to the way Baptists support missions? In what ways does your church support international mission efforts? Efforts in your state? Local efforts?

Challenges for Missions. Ask, Of the challenges to missions from within the Baptist denomination that are mentioned in the leaflet, which one do you think is the most serious? Why? How do materialism, relativism, and universalism adversely affect missions? What suggestions do you have to counter these challenges to Christian missions? [Note: In advance of the group meeting, you may find it helpful to do a study of materialism, relativism, and universalism and be prepared to share with the group a summary description of these since the words are not in the everyday vocabulary of many persons.]

In other countries and cultures, mission efforts by missionaries from America and Europe have been criticized in various ways, such as that they are part of Western colonialism, they disrupt native cultures, and they are expressions of Christian arrogance and intolerance of other religions. Ask, What are some answers to such criticisms?

Closing

Ask, How are Baptist mission efforts related to basic Baptist beliefs, such as the Lordship of Christ, the authority of the Bible, the priesthood of all believers, salvation only by grace through faith in Christ, and evangelism? Lead the members of the group in reviewing the Fill in the Blanks section and the Application Questions in the *Personal Study Guides* book.

Prayer Time

Mention the specific mission activities of your church and the names of persons involved in these and request someone to lead in prayer for these activities and persons.

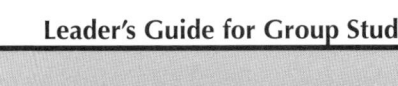
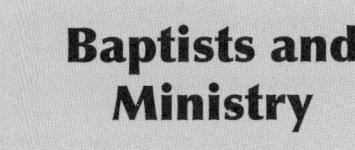

Baptists and Ministry

The following suggestions for leaders of group study are based on Baptist Identity Leaflet No. 16.

Scripture Memory

"Inasmuch as ye have done it unto one of the least of these my brethren, ye have done it unto me." Matthew 25:40

Getting Started

Begin the meeting with prayer. Request the group to read in unison the scripture in the center section of the leaflet that is printed across the Bibles (Matthew 25:40) and that is also printed in the Scripture Memory section above and in the *Personal Study Guides* book. Lead the group to memorize this scripture passage.

Indicate that Charles Hadden Spurgeon was one of the most famous Baptist pastors of all time. He pastored in London in the 1800s, and he was known for evangelistic preaching and also for the many ministries to needy persons by the church that he pastored, thus combining evangelism and ministry. Then read aloud the quote from him on the front page of the leaflet.

Guiding the Group Study

Lead a discussion on each of the subsections of the leaflet. Here are some suggested discussion starters, or you may choose to develop your own.

Bases for Ministry. In a format large enough for the group to read, list each of the basic Baptist beliefs discussed in the leaflet. Then lead a discussion about the relation of each of these to ministry. For instance, in regard to the basic belief in the Lordship of Christ you might discuss how both the actions and teachings of the Lord Jesus indicate the significant importance of ministry. In the leaflet a number of scriptures are referenced that illustrate how Jesus set an example of ministering to all kinds of persons and caring for their physical, mental and emotional, social, and spiritual needs. In advance of the meeting, print out the scripture passages that are referenced, each one on a card or piece of paper, and distribute these at the meeting to the members. Request the members to read these aloud one at a time as you reference the particular need that the passage relates to.

Extent of Ministry. In a format large enough for the group to read, draw columns headed by the following terms: "Physical Needs," "Mental and Emotional Needs," "Social Needs," and "Spiritual Needs."

Request the members of the group to give specific examples of possible ministries related to each of the needs listed and write these in the appropriate columns. Then request the members to cite examples of Baptist ministry to the various kinds of people listed in the leaflet. Then request the members to mention specific Baptist ministries in the places that the leaflet lists. Ask, Which ministries are carried out by your church? [Note: Be prepared to provide examples of ministries carried out by your church, of Baptist ministries to various kinds of people, and of Baptist ministries in a variety of places in case the members are not familiar with these.]

Methods of Ministry. Lead the group to state specific examples of the methods that Baptists utilize to deliver ministries. [Note: Be prepared to supply examples for each of these methods in case the members are not familiar with them.] Request the members to indicate which, if any of these methods, they are personally involved in.

> Case Study. A deacon in a Baptist church proposes that the church organize a group in the church to provide minor repairs and maintenance for the homes of persons who are unable to care for these on their own. The idea meets resistance from some of the church members who raise a number of concerns, such as liability, who determines which persons are to receive such service, possible complaints from those who are not helped, potential objections from businesses that "sell" such services, expense, and the like. Ask, What do you think the church should do? If you believe that the ministry should be carried out, what process would you recommend to deal with these concerns?

Closing

One of the challenges in carrying out ministries is that the number of ministry needs is often overwhelming. There is no way that any one person, church, or denomination can meet all of the needs. Ask, In light of the huge number of ministry needs, how can a church determine which ones it should strive with God's help to meet? How can an individual determine which ones he or she should strive to meet? How can a denomination determine which ministry needs it should endeavor to meet? Lead the members of the group in reviewing the Fill in the Blanks section and the Application Questions in the *Personal Study Guides* book.

Prayer Time

Request the members of the group to share specific prayer requests related to ministries that are being carried out by their church and pray for these.

Baptists and Christian Education

The following suggestions for leaders of group study are based on Baptist Identity Leaflet No. 17.

Scripture Memory

*"The fear of the Lord is the beginning of knowledge:
but fools despise wisdom and instruction."* Proverbs 1:7

Getting Started

Begin the meeting with prayer. Then have the group read in unison the scripture printed on the inside of the leaflet (Proverbs 1:7) that is also printed in the Scripture Memory section above and in the *Personal Study Guides* book. Lead the group in memorizing the scripture passage.

Briefly share with the group the beginning of Baptist college education in America. Because of their religious beliefs, Baptists were among those not allowed to attend the first schools that were established in America. Baptists played a major role in founding the colony of Rhode Island, and one of the features of the colony was its provision for religious freedom. Therefore, Baptists were free to establish a school in Rhode Island that would practice religious freedom. They established the College of Rhode Island, which today is Brown University. In succeeding years Baptists began many schools throughout America.

Read aloud the statement found in the box on the first page of the leaflet. Indicate that what George W. Truett said decades ago has been partially fulfilled, but much yet needs to be done. Ask, Do you believe that the Baptist denomination is generally perceived as a "teaching denomination"? What is the basis for your answer? What are some factors that demonstrate the Baptist commitment to Christian education in general? To Christian higher education in universities and seminaries?

Guiding the Group Study

Lead a discussion on each of the subsections of the leaflet. Here are some suggested discussion starters, or you may choose to develop your own.

Reasons for Baptist Support of Christian Education. Ask, Why should Christian education include a study of things other than the Bible? Indicate that many Baptist universities state that they "integrate faith and learning." Ask, What do you think is meant by this statement? How does Christian education strengthen churches as well as society in general?

The Relation of Christian Education to Other Baptist Principles. Ask, In what way does Christian education strengthen understanding of Baptist beliefs and polity and in turn how do Baptist beliefs and polity contribute to Christian education? If a Baptist university does not emphasize Baptist beliefs and practices, how does this weaken the effort of Baptists in fulfilling the Great Commission (Matthew 28:18-20) and the Great Commandment (Matthew 22:37-39)?

Kinds of Christian Education. Indicate that when the term "Christian education" is used, many people think only in terms of Christian higher education, such as that in Baptist universities and seminaries. Ask, Why is that too narrow a concept of Christian education, as important as the contributions of these institutions are? Do you believe that Christian education for vocational church leadership should be different from that for laypersons? If you believe it should be different, in what ways should it be?

Methods of Christian Education. Request members to share ways in which they have benefited from the various methods and delivery systems mentioned in the leaflet.

Challenges Related to Christian Education. Ask, In what way is your church contributing to the Christian education of its members? How can the members of the church become more supportive and involved? What can your church do to enhance Christian education throughout the Baptist denomination? What can you personally do to strengthen Baptist Christian education? Indicate that a number of universities once close to the Baptist denomination have weakened or severed that relationship. Ask, What are the dangers in this trend? How can Baptists maintain a strong presence in Christian higher education?

Closing

Many formerly distinctively Christian schools that had a strong denominational relation have lost that relation and have become basically secular private schools. This is a danger among Baptist schools. Ask, How can your church and each of us help to maintain schools that are distinctively Christian and unapologetically Baptist? Lead the members of the group in reviewing the Fill in the Blanks section and the Application Questions in the *Personal Study Guides* book.

Prayer Time

Request the members to pray silently for the following: for the many efforts by Baptists to provide Christian education, for the persons in leadership positions in Christian education, for the prayerful and financial support needed to increase this vital aspect of Baptist life, and for personal involvement in strengthening Christian education.

Baptists:
Applying the Gospel

The following suggestions for leaders of group study are based on Baptist Identity Leaflet No. 18.

Scripture Memory

"…And what does the Lord require of you? To act justly and to love mercy and to walk humbly with your God." Micah 6:8 (NIV)

Getting Started

Begin the meeting with prayer. Enlist a person to read the scripture as printed in the center of the leaflet (Micah 6:8) that is also printed in the Scripture Memory section above and in the *Personal Study Guides* book. Lead the group in memorizing the passage.

Indicate that some persons believe that Christians should major solely on evangelism and not be involved in activities to correct wrongs in society. Billy Graham, one of the best known evangelists of all time, emphasized the importance of both. Read aloud the quote by Billy Graham on the first page of the leaflet and indicate that this study shows why many other Baptists agree with his statement.

Ask, What is the difference between Christian ministry and Christian social action? Request the group to give specific examples of each. [Hint: Caring for persons made ill by toxic wastes from a manufacturing plant is ministry; bringing pressure on the owners of the plant to clean up the toxic wastes is social action.] Ask, How are Christian ministry and Christian social action related to one another in a beneficial way?

Guiding the Group Study

Lead a discussion on each of the subsections of the leaflet. Here are some suggested discussion starters, or you may choose to develop your own.

Bases for Applying the Gospel. Ask, How do the beliefs in the Lordship of Christ and in the authority of the Bible undergird a commitment to Christian social action? What are some specific problems in our country that Jesus as Lord and the teachings of the Bible indicate are violations of God's will for a just and loving society? List those that are mentioned in a format large enough for the group to read. Ask, What are Baptists doing to correct these problems?

Methods of Applying the Gospel. Ask, How are evangelism and social action interrelated? What are some of the methods that your church has used to right wrongs in society?

Case Study. A store in the neighborhood near a church is selling pornographic material, even to minors. The police are doing little to stop the activity. A member of the church in a business meeting makes a motion that the church organize a boycott of the store. Ask, Do you believe that this is appropriate action for a church? What might be objections to it? What are the difficulties in carrying it out?

Challenges to Applying the Gospel. Ask, Why does applying the gospel often take unusual courage? Which of the social problems that have been identified in this session would be the most dangerous for persons trying to correct them? What are some examples of persons who exhibited unusual courage to right a social wrong? [Note: Be prepared to give examples if members of the group cannot.] What would you say to counter those who insist that social action is either a waste of time or something that churches should not be involved in?

Case Study. A Baptist pastor helps to organize a statewide group to oppose gambling interests, and he begins to receive threats. Some of the members of the church where he is pastor protest his involvement, saying that his time should be spent on more spiritual matters. Ask, What role do you think a church should play in dealing with such social problems?

Closing

Ask, How does the Great Commandment of Jesus (Matthew 22:37-39) regarding love for God and for others relate to ministry and the application of the gospel? Briefly summarize the Baptist struggles for religious freedom for all persons as an example of the application of the gospel in actions to right a wrong in society. Lead the members of the group in reviewing the Fill in the Blanks section and the Application Questions in the *Personal Study Guides* book.

Prayer Time

Guide a silent prayer time, requesting the members to pray for the following: that every church will develop a genuine concern to combat social injustices, that each church and the Baptist denomination as a whole will become more involved in correcting social ills, and that persons will be willing to be involved in these efforts even if the cost is great.

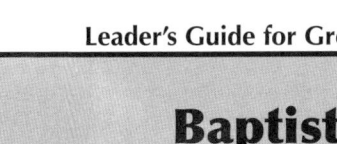

Baptists

Champions of Religious Freedom

The following suggestions for leaders of group study are based on Baptist Identity Leaflet No. 19.

Scripture Memory

"…ye have been called unto liberty; only use not liberty for an occasion to the flesh, but by love serve one another." Galatians 5:13

Getting Started

Begin the meeting with prayer. Request the group to read in unison the scripture printed at the top of the leaflet (Galatians 5:13) that is also printed in the Scripture Memory section above and in the *Personal Study Guides* book. Then lead the group in memorizing the passage.

Indicate that many historians credit Baptists with being in the forefront of efforts for religious freedom. A reason for this Baptist commitment to religious freedom is that it relates to all basic Baptist beliefs. Read aloud the statement by William R. Estep on the back page of the leaflet. This study is about the strong commitment of Baptists to religious freedom.

Request the group to read in unison the quotation from George Bancroft in the introductory paragraph of the leaflet. Indicate that the goal by Baptists for religious freedom was founded on basic biblical principles. Ask, What other motives or rationale could persons have for wanting religious freedom?

Guiding the Group Study

Lead a discussion on each of the subsections of the leaflet. Here are some suggested discussion starters, or you may choose to develop your own.

The Bases for Religious Freedom. Request members to share personal experiences they have had with each of the five freedoms mentioned in this section of the leaflet. Lead a discussion on the relation of each of these freedoms to basic Baptist beliefs, such as the Lordship of Christ, the authority of the Bible, regenerate church membership, congregational church governance, church autonomy, and evangelism.

The Struggle for Religious Freedom. Summarize briefly the early history of Christianity in Europe and North America stressing the close relation of church and state that existed. Ask, Why did government leaders, such as kings and princes, often want a close relationship with one of the Christian denominations, such as Roman Catholicism, Church of England,

and Lutheran? Why were many leaders of these denominations willing to partner with government authorities? Why did both government and religious leaders persecute those who held beliefs and practices contrary to the government-supported denomination? In addition to persecution, what are some of the other harmful consequences of the close relation of church and state?

Baptists and Religious Freedom through Separation of Church and State. Share briefly who George W. Truett was and have the group read in unison the quotation by him in the last paragraph of the preceding section of the leaflet, "The Struggle for Religious Freedom." Ask, What is the relation of church-state separation to religious freedom? Why is it important to emphasize that the separation should be friendly? Request members to share information about persons mentioned in this section of the leaflet. [Note: It would be helpful prior to the group meeting to familiarize yourself with these historic Baptist figures.]

The Application of Religious Freedom. Request members to share specific ways in which each of the responses to religious freedom could be carried out. Ask, What are some examples of the lack of religious freedom in some other nations? Why do persons in the United States of America enjoy more religious freedom than people of many other nations have? Why have Baptists been willing to sacrifice for religious freedom for all persons, not just for themselves? Request the group to read in unison again the scripture at the beginning of the leaflet (Galatians 5:13) and indicate that freedom is not something to be selfishly enjoyed but something to aid in serving others. Then ask the group to name specific ways our freedom can be used to serve or help others and list these in a format large enough for the group to read.

Closing

Indicate that while Baptists regard religious freedom as something good to be strived for and preserved, many persons and groups regard it as something dangerous to be restricted or eliminated. The latter view prevailed in Europe and America in the past and continues to do so in many parts of the world. Ask, In light of the opposition of many to religious freedom, why should Baptists continue to strive to provide it for all persons? Lead the members of the group in reviewing the Fill in the Blanks section and the Application Questions in the *Personal Study Guides* book.

Prayer Time

Request the members to close their eyes and reflect about the opportunities and responsibilities afforded by religious freedom and then to pray for guidance from and empowerment by the Holy Spirit in striving to provide religious freedom for all persons.

The *Baptist Identity Series* is intended to provide general, concise material on Baptist beliefs and heritage, not an in-depth study. Volumes of in-depth material exist on Baptist beliefs.

Encourage those interested in further study to use www.baptistdistinctives.org for a wealth of information and links to other resources.

About the *Baptist Identity Series*

Concern! Vision! Action! Cooperation! Results!

These words describe how the *Baptist Identity Series* came about.

Concern. A dedicated Baptist layman and active churchman, Noble Hurley, became quite concerned about the diminishing understanding by Baptists and others of basic Baptist beliefs and practices. Aware of the contributions by Baptists to the mission of the Lord Jesus Christ, he was concerned that a lack of knowledge about and commitment to Baptist beliefs would lead to erosion of the Baptist contributions to the cause of Christ and to the world in general. He was not alone in his concern.

Vision. A person of vision, Hurley believed that widespread informative and inspirational materials about Baptists as related to biblical truth could be used to increase understanding of what Baptists believe and practice.

Action. He acted to make such materials a reality. He realized that Baptists hold no monopoly on truth and did not want to disparage any other denomination. However, he wanted to perpetuate the Baptist beliefs and practices which had benefited multitudes of persons through centuries. To this end he asked William M. Pinson, Jr. and Doris A. Tinker to prepare the materials and provided funds to publish the materials.

Cooperation. As work began on the preparation of materials on Baptist identity, many persons, including pastors, historians, theologians, and Sunday School teachers, were enlisted to assist in a variety of ways. The materials first appeared as colorful articles in the *Baptist Standard*. A website was developed for the articles, resources, and other information. The positive response to the articles led to the development of the *Baptist Identity Series* that was made possible by the cooperative efforts of many.

Results. The many requests for the articles to be available in leaflet form led to the development of nineteen Baptist Identity Leaflets in a colorful 4-page 5.5 x 8.5 format. In order to enhance the usefulness of the leaflets, a book of nineteen study guides was prepared for use by persons in individual and/or group study of the leaflets. Also, a book was developed for persons leading group studies containing study guides on the nineteen leaflets along with suggestions for leading the studies. Requests for the leaflets to also be available in a book led to the development of *Baptist Beliefs and Heritage*, an 11 x 8.5 volume that contains a summary of Baptist history, a section of quotations on the Baptist commitment to religious freedom, the nineteen Baptist Identity Leaflets, and a page preceding each leaflet containing biographical sketches of Baptist leaders, insights on key words and terms used in the materials, historical vignettes, and brief accounts of persons and events in Baptist heritage. Thus, the *Baptist Identity Series* consists of these items: three books—*Personal Study Guides, Leader's Guide for Group Study, Baptist Beliefs and Heritage*—and nineteen individual Baptist Identity Leaflets.

Contributors to the
Baptist Identity Series

Material Preparation

Many persons cooperated in the development of the materials of the *Baptist Identity Series*. The following were the primary contributors:

William M. Pinson, Jr. authored the materials in the *Baptist Identity Series*. He has served as a seminary professor, pastor, interim pastor in Texas, Kansas, and New York, president of Golden Gate Baptist Seminary in California, executive director of the Baptist General Convention of Texas (BGCT), and member of various commissions of the Baptist World Alliance. He has taught and written extensively on Baptists.

Doris A. Tinker served as the primary designer for the *Series* leaflets and books, assisted in research and editing, and coordinated the entire project. She has served as a volunteer in Baptist churches in Arkansas, Illinois, and Texas, pastor's secretary, long-time executive associate in the BGCT executive director's office, communications/organization director of the Texas Baptist Heritage Center, and facilitator for many meetings on Baptist identity.

Dennis A. Parrott provided valuable input for the personal and group study guides. He has served as minister of education in a number of Baptist churches and as the director of the Bible study department of the BGCT. He has authored curriculum material for various Baptist publications.

Skyler G. Tinker assisted in developing the graphics and layout for the leaflets and the study guides. He comes from a deep Baptist background and has been part of a Baptist church all of his life. He graduated from the University of Texas at Dallas majoring in arts and technology with a minor in computer science.

Others, such as the following, contributed in various ways. Stephanie and Aaron Beazley, each a part of generations of strong Baptist families, assisted in editing materials and preparing them for printing and also contributed to updating the website www.baptistdistinctives.org. Debbie O'Toole, Sunday School teacher and Baptist pastor's daughter, provided consultation as representative of the company that printed the *Series*. Looie Biffar, long-time Baptist denominational worker, provided technical assistance.

Financial Assistance

A number of individuals and entities, including the following, embraced the vision of the *Baptist Identity Series* and contributed financially, making the materials available at very reasonable costs: The Jane and Noble Hurley Baptist Identity Fund, Bill and Ruth Landes Pitts through the James and Irene Landes Memorial Fund, Vester T. Hughes, Jr., and The Prichard Family Foundation.

How to Order Materials
in the
Baptist Identity Series

For current information on ordering, including price and shipping information, see the website www.baptistdistinctives.org.

The *Baptist Identity Series* is made up of the following items:

1. ***Baptist Beliefs and Heritage***—an 11 x 8.5 book that contains the Baptist Identity Leaflets,* a summary of Baptist history, biographical sketches of Baptist leaders, insights on key words and terms in the *Series*, historical vignettes, and pertinent information on each of the nineteen leaflets related to Baptist heritage.

> * Baptist Identity Leaflets—a set of nineteen colorful leaflets in a 4-page 5.5 x 8.5 format on Baptist beliefs and practices on which the study guides are based. As indicated above they are in the bound copy of the *Baptist Beliefs and Heritage* book. They are also available in a packet containing all nineteen leaflets.

2. ***Personal Study Guides***—a 5.5 x 8.5 book containing nineteen guides for use by persons in individual or group study on the topics in the Baptist Identity Leaflets.

3. ***Leader's Guide for Group Study***—a 5.5 x 8.5 book for leaders of study groups containing guides for each of the leaflets on the topics in the Baptist Identity Leaflets.

The following information may be helpful in ordering:

The ***Baptist Beliefs and Heritage*** book is helpful for anyone wishing to learn about Baptist identity. It is especially designed for use by persons studying the Baptist Identity Leaflets either as an individual or as part of a group. The book would be an ideal gift to a new church member or to someone interested in becoming a member of a Baptist church.

The ***Personal Study Guides*** book is a companion to the *Baptist Beliefs and Heritage* book. It is designed with learning activities for persons in studying the Baptist Identity Leaflets either as an individual or as part of a group.

The ***Leader's Guide for Group Study*** book is designed for persons who are leading groups in studying the Baptist Identity Leaflets or who are considering establishing or leading such groups. It contains suggested teaching guides for each of the nineteen leaflets. A person leading such a group as well as the members of the group will need to have both the *Baptist Beliefs and Heritage* book and the *Personal Study Guides* book.

The **Baptist Identity Leaflets** in the separate leaflet format can be used in a variety of ways, such as handouts in worship services or other meetings, resources for special events including baptismal services and the Lord's Supper, or as gifts to persons interested in knowing about Baptist beliefs.

Notes